POWER UP

An Hachette UK Company
www.hachette.co.uk

First published in Great Britain in 2023 by Godsfield,
an imprint of Octopus Publishing Group Ltd
Carmelite House, 50 Victoria Embankment, London EC4Y 0DZ
www.octopusbooks.co.uk

ISBN 978-1-8418-1534-3

A CIP catalogue record for this book is available from the British Library

Printed and bound in China

10 9 8 7 6 5 4 3 2 1

Publisher: Lucy Pessell
Designer: Isobel Platt
Senior Editor: Hannah Coughlin
Assistant Editor: Samina Rahman
Production Controller: Serena Savini

ALISON DAVIES

POWER UP

HOW TO BOOST YOUR ENERGY
LEVELS TO FEEL AWESOME

CONTENTS

Introduction

If you had to describe how you feel right now, what would you say? Do you feel energized and ready to embrace the day? Would you say you're a powerful presence in your own world, or just a bystander, trying to do the best you can? We all have off days, days when it feels we can do nothing right, and our strength is depleted. And we all have those amazing days when everything just seems to go right, when our mood is high, and our vitality even higher. It comes down to one thing, positive energy – having it, creating it, and holding on to it.

Positive energy is an attitude, it's a mindset, that makes you feel uplifted. It's that 'Yes!' moment when you feel on top of your game and ready for anything. And while it begins in the mind, it affects the body and how you feel. Your thoughts play an important role when it comes to how positive you are, but there are other things you can do to create more vim, vigour, and up those feel-good vibes.

This book shows you simple tricks and techniques that will help you feel more dynamic, invigorated, and empowered. You'll learn all about your aura, the life force which surrounds your body, and how to strengthen and protect it. You'll discover the power of affirmations and how meditation can help to centre you, so that you maintain a positive mindset. You'll learn breathing techniques that will boost energy, strength and personal power, and you'll also discover the magic of scripting, and how this can change your outlook for the better.

With exercises perfectly timed to fit in with your daily routine, and a sample plan, in the form of an energy clock that includes techniques to boost your positivity throughout your day, you'll understand how to lift yourself up, any time those dips occur. You'll also be given a selection of energy enhancers, little things you can do for an instant mood boost, while the chapter of the same name recommends other things you can use, like crystals, herbs, and scents, which will help you feel on top of the world.

Whether you're looking for inspiration, a change in your approach to each day, or just a way to feel more upbeat and energized, this little book has the answer. It's time to 'Power Up'. Embrace who you were meant to be and fill your life with positive energy.

AURA
WORK

1

What is an aura?

The Aura is the force field of energy which surrounds the body in colour and light. Imagine it like a shimmering layer of protection which frames you from head to toe in a myriad of hues. Generally, someone who is feeling energized will have a strong aura which extends outwards and surrounds them in bright light. This aura will be filled with shades of colour, which represent how they're feeling at any given moment. For example, someone who has a lot of red in their aura, might be feeling angry or passionate, while someone with patches of purple around their head, might be in an intuitive mood.

While it's invisible to most, some energy workers can see the aura with practice and even read the different colours and decipher their meaning. Even if you can't see the aura yourself, you will be able to sense it, and also feel when its depleted. It reflects how you're feeling inside and out, so it makes sense that you can boost your mood and vitality by changing the way your aura looks and feels.

There are many techniques to help you do this, but the most effective combine visualization with focused breathing to extend the range and brightness.

MY AURA SHINES WITH BRIGHTNESS & STRENGTH

Turn up the Shine

Do this: First thing in the morning to give you energy and put you in a positive mindset for the day ahead. You can also do this any time when you need a boost, or to lift your mood.

You'll need: Nothing except the time and space to focus on your breathing and the visualization.

What to do:

1. Stand feet hip-width apart, shoulders relaxed.

2. Draw a deep breath in and imagine you're pulling it through the soles of your feet, along each leg and up into your stomach and chest.

3. As you exhale, release the breath into the air for four long beats.

4. Repeat the cycle of breathing for three or four more times, or until you feel calm and centred.

5. Now visualize a small dial, like a thermometer, in the centre of your chest. This dial controls the brightness and strength of your aura.

6. As you draw the breath in, imagine the dial turning upwards to increase the power and energy.

7. As you release the breath, picture your aura getting bigger and brighter. See it extending outwards and feel the vibrancy of its shine.

8. Continue to turn the dial upwards with every breath and focus on the aura getting bolder as you exhale.

9. To finish, place both hands over the centre of your chest, palms down. Feel the heat beneath your fingers and say (aloud or silently depending on the situation) 'My aura shines with brightness and strength.'

Energy Enhancer

Depending on how you feel and what you'd like to achieve during your day, you can infuse your aura with different colours. Each one has a particular meaning and attribute.

On the next page is a key that you can use to pick the right shade. All you have to do, is repeat the exercise above and visualize your aura shining brightly in the colour of your choice.

Aura colour guide

White	Purity, Energy, Vitality
Gold	Power, Confidence, Energy
Silver	Clarity, Freedom, Focus
Purple	Intuition, Psychic Power, Individuality
Pink	Love, Kindness, Empathy
Red	Passion, Tenacity, Assertiveness
Blue	Healing, Sensitivity, Strength
Green	Growth, Creativity, Balance
Yellow	Enthusiasm, Success, Luck
Orange	Joy, Radiance, Spontaneity
Turquoise	Wisdom, Tranquillity, Protection

Cleansing your aura

Like any part of your body, your aura gathers debris in the form of negativity, which not only dulls the shine but can cause blockages. When this happens the energy around your body does not flow freely, making you feel sluggish, and even under the weather. It's important to regularly cleanse your aura, just as you would your physical body. This will clear any pressure points where energy has built up and help you maintain a positive outlook.

Aura Spring Clean

Do this: At the beginning of the weekend when you're relaxing. It will help to eliminate any negative energy that you've collected during the week, so that you can enjoy your days off and feel rejuvenated. You can also perform it any time you feel off kilter, it will help to restore balance and put a spring in your step.

You'll need: A feather, some sage essential oil, and a small bowl of hot water.

What to do:

1. Half fill the bowl with boiling water and add in five drops of sage essential oil. If you prefer, you can use the fresh herb and let it steep in the water for five minutes.

2. Lean over the bowl and let the scent of the sage fill you up. Breathe deeply and enjoy the freshness of the aroma.

3. Place the bowl on a table next to you, and take the feather, let it waft some of the scented steam up over your head.

4. Flick the feather forward and back in the air around your body, as if you're flicking away any dust that has collected.

5. Start at the top of your head and work down each side of your body.

6. Go under each foot, by raising it in the air. Also be sure to do the space in front of your stomach, where negative energy can collect and weigh you down.

7. Picture your aura getting cleaner and brighter as you do this.

8. To finish say 'I cleanse my aura of negativity, let stagnant energy flow, as the obstacles go!'

Energy Enhancer

To really get the energy moving around your body, finish your aura cleanse with some body brushing. Start at your ankles and be sure to brush upwards towards your heart. As you do, continue to visualize your aura looking clean and bright. Imagine any blockages are being brushed away and feel the revitalizing energy flood your entire body. You will probably notice that as your skin tingles and brightens, your mood lifts and you feel infused with vitality.

Protecting your aura

When you are feeling under the weather or lacking in energy it's a clear sign your aura is depleted. This can happen as a result of illness, stress, and over-work, or it can be related to other external factors, like spending time with people who drain you, or taking on the emotions and problems of others.

While it's natural to experience dips in energy at stressful times, you can protect your aura from outside influence, which in turn will boost energy reserves and help you deal with external circumstances from a place of power.

Put up an Aura Shield

Do this: First thing in the morning, to protect your aura throughout the day. You can also do this whenever you feel vulnerable. It will help to keep negative emotions and energy at bay.

You'll need: A quiet moment where you won't be disturbed to set this up, but once you get into the habit of doing this, you'll be able to create your shield almost instantly.

What to do:

1. Take a deep breath in to centre yourself.

2. Draw the air up through your feet and legs, into your stomach.

3. Feel it fill your chest and travel up your neck and then exhale with a long breath out of your mouth.

4. Continue to breathe in this way, so that you create a continual loop of air moving in and out.

5. When you inhale imagine a shield of light rising up, over the front of your body, over the top of your head and down the other side. See it form a golden cocoon, which completely covers you.

6. With every breath you take, the cocoon solidifies, and the golden light becomes brighter.

7. Imagine it as a Teflon type substance which rebuffs negative energy.

8. Whilst you are within the cocoon, you are protected from any external influences that might leave you feeling drained of energy. You can go about your daily business, without taking on the negative emotions of others.

9. Continue to re-enforce the cocoon at any point during the day, when you feel your energy waning. Simply, imagine you're encased in golden light, and see it extending outwards.

Keeping your aura clean and bright is an on-going process, and there are simple tricks and tips that you can use to help. Being mindful of your own thoughts is a good starting point. Being negative with yourself, will cloud your aura and dampen down the shine, so whenever you hear the inner critic surfacing, say 'stop!' and replace the negative thought with something positive and empowering.

Also be mindful of your interactions with others. If you notice that someone leaves you feeling drained, or tends to dump their emotional baggage on you, put some boundaries in place. Only see this person when you feel in the right headspace to deal with them, and always be sure to put up your 'aura shield' before you meet.

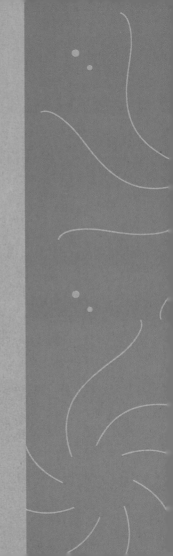

2

AFFIRMATIONS AND MANTRAS

What are affirmations?

Affirmations are positive statements. They are sentences which describe how you feel in the present moment, and they are created to banish negativity, and reprogram the way you think. Used in combination with other tools like meditation and visualization, they're incredibly powerful, and can rewire the brain. You can use them anytime, and depending on where you are, you can either repeat them out loud or in your head to focus the mind and switch up your thinking.

The key is to speak them in the present, rather than putting them in future. For example, if you say, 'I will feel full of energy.' You are putting the 'energy' part in the future and creating distance between yourself and your goal. What you are actually saying is 'this will happen, but not yet'.

If you say, 'I am full of energy.' Then it's happening right now. You bring it closer by bringing it into your present moment which eliminates any distance.

Even if you don't feel that way at the time, when you say an affirmation, you trick your mind into believing the words. By placing emphasis on the positive words and putting your emotions behind it you make it real, and the more you say it, the more you believe it, until eventually you feel it. Your mind becomes accustomed to thinking in a new and positive way, thus drowning out your inner critic – the nagging voice of self-doubt that continually puts you down.

Affirmations can be helpful when trying to adopt a brighter mindset. They can empower you and also encourage you to stay open to the flow of positive energy in your world.

Energizing Affirmations

* 'I step into my power and own it.'

* 'I am filled with light and love.'

* 'Everything I do, I do with vigour and vitality.'

* 'I embrace my best self today.'

* 'Each moment is an opportunity to be joyful.'

* 'Power seeps from every pore.'

* 'Today I am at my most vibrant.'

* 'I live in the moment, and the moment lives in me.'

* 'I am radiant, resilient, and ready!'

* 'I breath in energy, and release stress.'

Create Empowering Affirmations

Do this: At night, when you have the time to relax and reflect on the day that's gone.

You'll need: A pen and some paper.

What to do:

1. Start by centring yourself. Stand with your feet hip-width apart, your shoulders relaxed, and lengthen your spine.

2. Pull in your core as you inhale. Imagine drawing the breath through your feet, up through your body and over your head in a constant loop. Repeat this process for a couple of minutes.

3. Now get comfy with your paper and pen, and reflect on the day that's just gone.

4. What went well, and what didn't? If you had any standout moments when you felt great, recreate them in your mind. How did you feel at that time, sum this up in one or two words, so it might say, 'joyful' or 'loved'.

5. If things didn't go to plan, what would have helped? Think of one positive thing that might have helped you in the situation, for example, more 'courage', 'honesty', 'communication'?

6. Look at the words you have written and pick out the ones that resonate with you. You are drawn to these words for a reason, most likely because you need them in your life.

7. Consider how you can put them into an affirmation, so you might say, 'I am loved and joyful every day' or 'My courage grows with every breath I take.'

8. Experiment with the words and how you put them together – as long as you remember to keep them in the present, you can do anything with them.

9. Eventually you will find a phrase that feels right. This is your personal power affirmation.

Energy Enhancer

Affirmations grow and change, and while one might suit you and your situation right now, in a few weeks' time you might need something different.

Keep a note of the affirmations you create in a journal, and refresh them week by week, so that they meet your needs. Also record how effective they were.

Did they help you feel empowered, and if they didn't, why was this? Perhaps you didn't fully believe in the sentiment, or you forgot to repeat them regularly.

What are mantras?

Mantras are words or sounds that can be used to focus the mind, deepen the meditative state, and effect your physical and mental wellbeing. Over time, and when used often, they can alter your perception and generate energy, depending on what you focus on. For example, you could choose a sound like 'Om', which deeply resonates with your inner psyche, and brings balance and peace, or you could choose a word like 'Love' and repeat that.

The key is to focus on what the word means to you, as you repeat it in your mind or out loud. If you're using a sound, then you connect with the vibrations as it reverberates through your system. Like a tuning fork, the sound gives your mind something to focus on, which helps you relax and centre yourself.

Power Up Mantra

Do this: At any point in the day, when you have five minutes to yourself. Some people do find it helpful to set a specific time aside every day, so that they get into a habit of working with the mantra, this is usually first thing in the morning, or later in the evening.

You'll need: A space where you are comfortable, and you won't be disturbed. To help induce a sense of calm, you might want to light candles or burn scented oil like geranium, which balances the body and mind.

What to do:

1. Sit in a comfortable position. Lengthen your spine, and let your shoulders relax so that your diaphragm is able to move freely, and you can take deep breaths.

2. Place your hands, palm upwards at either side on your lap, or knees depending on your sitting position.

3. Close your eyes and focus on the word 'Power'. Think of it as an energizing force that fills you with positive energy and allows you to be yourself. When you are imbued with

power, you are strong, revitalized, and ready for anything.

4. Draw a deep breath in and as you exhale, say the word, extending each syllable and vowel.

5. Let the word resonate in your chest and linger upon your tongue, as you release your breath.

6. Repeat this process, and each time you exhale, let the word sing from your soul. You may find that it gets louder and more vibrant each time.

7. Enjoy the sound of the word and notice how it matches the meaning.

8. Do this for five minutes, then open your eyes; stand up slowly and give your body a shake to get the energy flowing.

Energy Enhancer

When you work with mantras, you're engaging your mind and also your senses, as you not only 'hear' the word, but also 'taste' it on your tongue. Go a step further and bring in your sense of 'sight' by thinking of an image that conjures a feeling of 'Power' in your mind. If it helps, draw or sketch something, or put together a collage using pictures from magazines. Using visual cues, along with the word and breathing exercise, enhances the strength of the mantra and its meaning for you. It's also handy to have a visual prompt that you can leave somewhere obvious, as a reminder of what you're trying to create.

BREATHWORK

3

Energy and breathing

The calming power of a few deep breaths is obvious.
It lowers the heart rate and helps to control the release
of the stress hormone, which in turn makes you feel more
relaxed and centred. As you increase the amount of
oxygen you take in, your mind will clear. This triggers the
release of endorphins, which have a feel-good effect on
the body.

Deep breathing helps in other ways too. It oxygenates the
blood, giving you an instant lift and boosting blood flow so
that you have more energy. It balances the emotions and
also stimulates the lymphatic system which helps to de-
toxify the body, and it has a similar effect on the mind too.

Scientists recognize that there's a direct link between the
way you breathe and your autonomic nervous system, and
if you alter the way you breathe and employ some clever
techniques, you'll instantly feel more empowered and
energized. You'll also be more engaged because you're
paying attention to the life force that enters your body.
You'll be present in the moment, and this will make you
feel more alive and impactful.

What is breathwork?

Breathwork looks specifically at how you breathe, and how to make your breathing more effective by employing tried and tested techniques. It combines the power of the mind, with the power of the body, and is particularly effective when it comes to controlling the emotions and helping you maintain a positive outlook.

It's all about paying attention to the way you breathe, which is something that doesn't come naturally to us in the Western world. We tend to rush through our days, trying to get as much done as possible, taking short, sharp, shallow breaths, and in some cases withholding our breath altogether. This makes the body think it's under threat, and so it responds by going into 'fight or flight' mode and creating even more tension.

When you become aware of your breath, and the effect that it has, you can work with it to create positive energy, and step into your power. You can ensure that you're breathing correctly by being present and checking in with your body throughout the day, and by doing so, you'll know how to maximize each inhalation and tailor it to suit your energy needs.

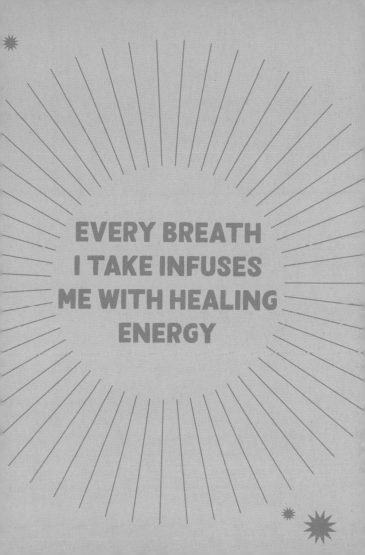

The Calming Breath

Do this: Whenever you need to take some time out and to calm your thoughts. This is also a great exercise to do before bed, as it will soothe you into sleep.

You'll need: A few minutes to yourself. Depending on the situation, if you're using the calming breath to help you sleep, you might want to put on some soothing music, or dab lavender essential oil on your temples.

What to do:

1. Relax, and breathe in through your nose. Be sure to keep your mouth shut as you inhale, this is all about filtering the air through your nostrils.

2. Make sure the breath is long and deep, and hold for the count of four slow beats.

3. Exhale through your mouth, releasing the breath gradually. This is not forceful; it's a gentle exhalation and you want it to last for four long beats.

4. Repeat the breath, taking your time and drawing it in deeply through your nose. This time hold the breath for five long beats.

5. Exhale gradually through the mouth and make it last for five beats.

6. Repeat the process again, and this time see if you can hold the breath for six beats and do the same as you exhale.

7. The key is to take your time, this is slow breathing which should be soothing, and will also give your mind something simple to focus on.

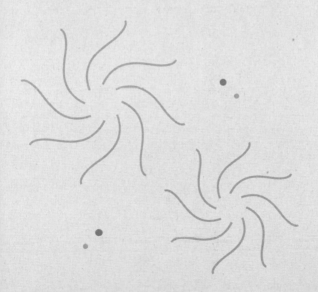

Energy Enhancer

As you perform the energizing breath routine and take the breaths in quick succession, imagine you're using a bike pump to inflate your lungs with air. You might even want to visualize a pump in the centre of your chest. Feel it inflating with every breath. This action generates energy and will increase the power of each breath that you take, which boosts your vitality. Always ensure you break the routine with five normal breaths, otherwise you might feel lightheaded.

The Energizing Breath

Do this: Anytime that you need an energy boost.
This is particularly good before a workout, as it
will imbue you with strength and give you the
momentum you need to reach any fitness goals.

You'll need: A bottle of chilled water to sip after
you've completed the breathing routine.

What to do:

1. Sit or stand in a comfortable position. Take a sharp deep
   breath in through your nose, keeping your mouth closed.

2. Exhale in a short burst, through pursed lips so that you
   make a 'swooshing' sound.

3. Repeat five times in a quick succession, then relax and
   breathe normally for five breaths.

4. Repeat the routine again. These breaths should only take a
   couple of seconds each time.

5. Relax and take five normal breaths.

6. To finish, repeat the whole routine for six breaths.

7. Give your body a good shake to get the energy circulating
   through your system and take a couple of sips of water.

The Powerful Breath

Do this: Before a big event, or at any point when you're feeling vulnerable and need to generate powerful energy.

You'll need: Space to move freely, where you won't be disturbed for a couple of minutes.

What to do:

1. Stand with your feet hip-width apart.

2. Roll your shoulders back and tilt your chin upwards slightly.

3. Let your arms hang down, but bring the tips of your fingers together, palms turned upwards.

4. Draw a long slow breath in and as you do, bring your palms up until they are level with your chest. Imagine you are lifting the breath upwards to sit in this area.

5. Hold the breath for a couple of beats, then turn your hands over, keeping the fingers tips together and extend them outwards in front of you, as you exhale.

6. This will look and feel like you're pushing the air away from you.

7. Extend your exhalation by a couple of beats. Then repeat

MY BREATH
IMBUES ME
WITH POWER
& STRENGTH

the breathing process, drawing the breath upwards, and then pushing it away from your body.

8. Imagine that the breath is your personal power. You draw it in, and then you put it out there for everyone to see and feel.

9. Repeat this for a few minutes, or until you feel more confident and empowered.

Other breathwork tips

Practice belly breathing Engage your belly for a deeper, more energizing breath. As you inhale, your stomach should move outwards. As you exhale, it should move in towards your spine.

Breathe mindfully Make it a habit to check in on your breath throughout the day. Notice if your chest feels tense, and how long and deep your breaths are. Stop at least three times a day and take a couple of deep breaths through your nose.

Inhale what you need Think of what you need and imagine that you're breathing it in, so if you want to feel strong, you might inhale the word 'Strength' with every breath.

Breathe through your nose The nose filters and humidifies the air you breathe. It's the healthiest way to breathe and allows the right amount of oxygen into your system, which in turn boosts vitality.

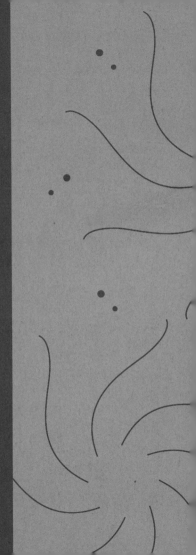

ENERGY ENHANCERS

4

What are energy enhancers?

Energy enhancers are things that can be used, either individually or alongside other techniques to increase your personal power and generate more positive energy. They help to maximize the flow of energy and enrich each exercise. They can relate to the senses like scents or flavours, or they can be of nature, and help to strengthen your bond with the natural world.

The energy enhancers in this chapter, stimulate the body and mind, and help to boost and maintain vitality. Think of them as key components of your energy toolkit. From crystals and stones to essential oils and herbs; there's a range of tools that you can choose from, depending on how you feel and what you need at any given time.

These enhancers can be used throughout the day, and they're easy to work with. Combine them with tricks, techniques, and rituals, to promote personal power, and help you feel on top form.

Crystals

Crystals can be used for healing, wellness and to boost the mood. They each have a specific type of energy, which you can work with. It's about finding the one that you're drawn to and deciding how best to connect with its power.

Citrine

Known as the 'cuddle quartz', this vibrant stone with its vivid golden hue is packed with positive energy. An instant mood booster, citrine works by raising your personal energy vibration and helping you look on the bright side. It promotes confidence and feel-good vibes, and is also thought to attract abundance, which is where it gets its mantel 'The Merchants Stone.'

Like attracts like in the realm of energy and this stone projects positivity, which in turn sends a powerful message to the Universe, to deliver more of the same.

Citrine Cuddle Cure

Do this: For a mid-afternoon lift, or any time when you're feeling under the weather.

You'll need: A small citrine cluster that you are drawn to and a couple of drops of tea-tree essential oil.

What to do:

1. Sprinkle a drop of tea tree oil into each palm, rub together lightly and cup your hands around the citrine.

2. Bring the stone towards the centre of your chest, where your heart chakra is situated, and hold here with both hands.

3. Spend a few moments breathing deeply, and as you do, imagine the golden light of the stone filling your chest and travelling through your entire body. Embrace the lightness of this energy and feel it surging through your system.

4. When you're ready, place the stone somewhere close, for example on your desk if you're at work, on a coffee table, or even in your pocket.

5. Rub your hands together one last time and feel the energy fizzing between your palms. Relax and breathe.

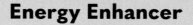

Energy Enhancer

One way to feel the healing benefits of any crystal is to make an energy infusion that you can sip throughout the day. You'll need some spring water, and the crystal of your choice. Pop the crystal in a jug, then cover with spring water. Place this in the refrigerator overnight. In the morning remove the crystal and decant the water into a bottle, so that you can sip it during the day. If you prefer, you can make ice cubes from the infused water, which you can add to your favourite juices and smoothies.

Quartz

Clear quartz, also known as Rock Crystal, is a beautiful vibrant stone that amplifies energy. It has the power to absorb negativity, and balance the body and mind. It is called a 'Master Healer' because of its ability to enhance the energy of other crystals. Thought to improve the memory, it also stimulates the immune system, and brings the body into balance, so it's the best choice if you're feeling emotionally drained.

A popular choice with mystics and healers who benefit from its intuitive properties, quartz is a great stone to carry with you at all times.

✹ ✹ Other Uplifting Crystals ✹ ✹

There are many crystals with uplifting, life affirming qualities, here are a few of the best for you to explore:

* ✳ Tiger's Eye
* ✳ Turquoise
* ✳ Carnelian
* ✳ Peridot
* ✳ Aventurine
* ✳ Bloodstone

Quartz Amplifier

....

Do this: To set your intention for the day and achieve a specific goal.

You'll need: A quartz crystal point, a piece of paper and a pen, and five minutes to focus your mind.

What to do:

1. Sit for a moment, with the crystal in both hands. Close your eyes and breathe deeply.

2. Focus on the rise and fall of your chest and clear your mind.

3. Now think about the day ahead, and what you hope to achieve. What qualities would help you do this? For example, you might choose clarity and strength to assist you if you're trying to solve a problem, or empathy and positivity, if you need to connect with someone.

4. Think about the qualities you have chosen. How would you sum them up in a picture or symbol? For example, you might choose a tree to represent strength or the sun to represent positive energy.

5. Once you have decided on your symbols, take the pen and paper, and have a go at drawing them, this doesn't need to be perfect, it's more about capturing the essence of the energy you require.

6. Place the paper on the floor in front of you and point the crystal towards the image. Take a deep breath in and feel a wave of energy surge through you. As you exhale, release that energy through the crystal point, into the symbol.

7. To finish, pop the crystal on top of the drawing and leave it there for at least five minutes.

8. When you're ready, retrieve the crystal and hold it at any point during the day, to restore focus.

I PRIORITIZE MY WELLBEING TO MAINTAIN A POSITIVE OUTLOOK

Herbs

Herbs are accessible, aromatic and packed with medicinal benefits. They're a natural way to stimulate immunity and lift the mood, and they're super easy to work with, whether you eat, brew, or burn them.

Sage

A cleansing herb, sage was used by the ancients to clear personal space of negative energy. It also stimulates the body and mind, so it's a great herb to work with if you want to boost your mental abilities.

Rosemary

In folklore rosemary is associated with powerful women, and used to cleanse, purify, and strengthen. It's the ideal choice for those moments when you need to boost your confidence and self-esteem.

Sage Morning Cleanser

Do this: To cleanse your body and mind for the day ahead and imbue you with positive energy.

You'll need: A handful of fresh sage, some honey and hot water.

What to do:

1. Steep the sage in a pan of boiling of water for five minutes.

2. Let it simmer, and then strain the liquid into a cup.

3. Add a spoonful of honey and stir while thinking about all the wonderful things you're going to achieve. Sip the infusion while setting your intentions.

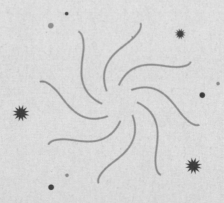

Rosemary Power Rinse

Do this: Whenever you wash your hair. Get into a regular routine of using this rinse to feel empowered and confident.

You'll need: Fresh sprigs of rosemary, hot water, and a jug.

What to do:

1. To begin, make the power rinse by steeping the rosemary sprigs in a pan of boiling water for ten minutes.

2. Let the mixture cool, then strain the liquid into a jug.

3. When you wash your hair, use the rinse after your shampoo and conditioner.

4. Turn your head upside down and pour it through your hair, then gently massage your scalp.

5. As you do this repeat this mantra, 'I am powerful, I am me. I am confident, I am free.'

6. Finish by rinsing your hair with warm water and styling as normal.

Essential Oils

These powerful oils are extracted from various parts of the wild plant to capture its essence. Made from different compounds that have been proven to help with healing and wellbeing, essential oils can be sniffed straight from the bottle or burnt in an oil burner. You can add a few drops to your bath water, or even mix with a carrier oil like almond or jojoba and use as a body lotion or massage oil.

Here's a list of some of the best oils for positive energy. Choose the one you like the smell of, and experiment using it in different ways.

* **Bergamot** Reduces stress and promotes a positivity
* **Orange** Alleviates anxiety and elevates the mood
* **Lemon verbena** Enhances focus and boosts energy
* **Geranium** Regulates the mood and calms the mind
* **Juniper** Cleanses body and mind, and lifts the emotions
* **Ylang Ylang** Boosts self-esteem and confidence
* **Frankincense** Reduces stress and generates positive energy
* **Peppermint** Stimulates the mind and boosts vitality

I CHOOSE VITALITY!

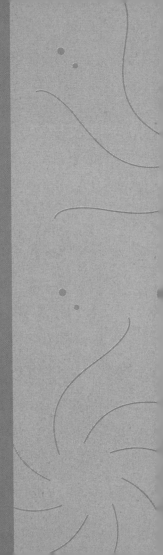

5 SCRIPT WORK & VISUALIZATION

What is script work?

Script work is a manifestation technique which uses stories to create reality as you'd like it to be. You become the author of your life, by describing what you'd like to happen. Scripting gives you the power to create anything you want by switching up the narrative, and the key is to bring it into the present. This means that when you write your script, you write as if it's happening now, rather than in the future.

Scripts don't have to be epic, they can be short paragraphs or tales, as long as they embody what you'd like to happen and bring it to life with words. You are the only person that needs to read what you have written, but you need to *connect* with the words on the page. Picture the scene as you read it, engage your emotions, then your script will be even more powerful, and likely to filter into your subconscious mind, which is the ultimate goal. The script helps to reframe your mindset, and establish beliefs and qualities that will help you achieve your goal. All you have to do is dream it, read it, and believe it.

You can create scripts for anything. They can be geared to a specific aim, for example, the holiday of a lifetime, or they can be more general, and can encompass a theme like generating positive energy, or feeling more powerful.

Positive Energy Script

Do this: At the beginning and end of every day to increase your positivity and help you find joy throughout the week.

You'll need: A pen and some paper.

What to do:

1. Spend some time thinking of things that make you feel positive, like your favourite fitness workout, or spending time with certain people. Perhaps you can think of one specific memory, when something happened that left you feeling super positive and uplifted.

2. Make a few notes of anything that comes to mind.

3. Look at what you've written and use it as inspiration for a short script to build positivity.

4. Start by writing *'today I feel on top of the world, I am brimming with energy as I get ready for work/the gym/to see my friends...I am excited because I am having fun and doing what I love. This makes me feel...'*

5. Fill in the blanks and put in as much detail and emotion as you can.

6. Start small like this and you can build up to bigger scripts, which include events and scenarios that make you feel positive.

7. When you've finished your paragraph, read it through a couple of times. As you do this, engage your senses – so see the gym in your mind, see the workout and hear your heart pumping, feel your muscles infused with strength and so on.

8. If you're reading the script in the evening, turn it around and imagine you're going out to meet friends, going to the gym, doing what you love after work.

9. Keep up the momentum of scripting by reading it a couple of times a day and adding to your script to make it even more authentic and powerful.

Energy Enhancer

Once you get into the habit of scripting, you'll find mini narratives pop into your head all the time, and it becomes natural to talk yourself into a positive frame of mind. You can encourage this even more by giving each script a theme tune, so you might choose your favourite upbeat track to create positive energy. To feel powerful, you might go for something more dramatic, perhaps a dancefloor tune that makes you want to take centre stage and throw some shapes. To feel centred, you might go for a soothing melody from childhood. As you get into the habit of bringing your scripts to life in this way, you'll find that you can conjure the feeling you want by bringing the theme tune to your mind. This then becomes a quick fix that you call upon at any time during the day.

What is visualization?

Visualization works with the potent power of images. It's about creating a series of pictures in your mind of what you'd like to happen. It's like watching a movie unfold, but instead of doing it on the big screen, you're doing it in your head. Again, the idea is that everything happens in the present and you experience all of the associated emotions at the same time. Visualization works well for people who like to think visually, and for those who might struggle with words. It's a simple process, and once you get the hang of it, a lot of fun. Basically, you're giving yourself permission to daydream, but with the added bonus that you're shaping reality.

You can create visualizations to help with anything, from forthcoming events to imagined scenarios. You can use them to manifest things like health, abundance and peace, or for specific situations that you'd like to invite into your life. They are a way of playing out events in your head in advance and planting the seeds of success.

Uplifting Visualization

Do this: When you need a boost. This visualization is the perfect pick-me-up and can be particularly effective at the beginning of a busy day.

You'll need: Space and time to sit and relax. If you can, find a spot to sit outside and feel the sun on your face, this will enhance the visualization.

The visualization:
Close your eyes and take a few deep breaths to calm your mind. Imagine you are sitting on the brow of the hill. It's the start of a new day, and the air is filled with promise. You take a deep breath in and enjoy the peace this brings. In the distance you can see the horizon. It shimmers as the first rays of sun dance into view. Down below the fern green valley stretches out before you, it's a landscape of peaks and troughs, as the earth curves and ripples. Slowly, steadily, the sun emerges, and the soft blue of the vista is tinged rose gold. The sky is alight with colours that blend into each other in waves. The land too is changing as dark becomes light, and the grass transforms into a sparkling emerald plateau. You drink it all in from your vantage point. You feel the breeze wrap around you, lifting you to

your feet. As you stand, stretch your arms wide open and embrace the scene before you. The sun wraps you up in a vibrant blanket of light and you feel alive, awakened, and full of hope.

I SEE, I BELIEVE, I AM

Personal Power Visualization

Do this: When you need to feel empowered. If you're feeling nervous, vulnerable or you just want to make a positive impression, this visualization should help. It's also a great exercise to practice the night before a big event.

You'll need: Time and space to relax, a seat by a window looking at the night sky.

The visualization:

If it's the evening, spend a few minutes looking at the night sky for inspiration.

Close your eyes and breathe deeply. You are laying on a warm dry blanket beneath the stars. The velvety sky presses down on you and there's a gentle breeze caressing your skin. As you gaze upwards, you can see a collection of twinkling stars, they glisten like diamonds against the inky backdrop. You can make out shapes and patterns within the constellations, and as you continue to stare, pictures begin to form. There is one star that stands out more than the others. It shimmers with such a brightness that you can't take your eyes off it. You instantly feel a connection, and as you watch closely, it seems that the star is moving closer. It is swooping through the heavens towards you.

Within seconds it is so close that you can almost touch it. The brightness takes over you, and you are no longer laying on the ground, you are part of the star; a shining white orb filling the sky with light. You can feel your brightness extending outwards. You can feel the power pulsating within you. With every breath, you grow stronger and stronger, until it feels like your light has absorbed everything around you.

Energy Enhancer

Visualizations are more flexible than scripts, and they will often move and change each time you perform them. Do not be afraid to let your mind wander and let the picture go in a different direction. It's important to engage your imagination and give yourself free rein to explore. When you do this, you connect at a deeper level, this makes the visualization even more effective.

MINDFUL MEDITATION

6

What is meditation?

Meditation is a way of transforming the mind and relaxing the body. It promotes a heightened state of awareness by using a number of different techniques which help to switch your focus and control your thoughts. A popular practice around the world, it can be used to find inner peace, and to release tension. There are many different types of meditation, some of which are spiritual and healing, and others which focus on reprogramming thought patterns, but the key with any form is to start slowly, and simply.

Meditation is not complicated. It's something that with a little effort, can help you achieve peace, harmony and balance, all of which generates more positive energy in your life. Couple this with some mindful techniques to bring you into the present moment, and you'll feel instantly energized and powerful.

Power Up Morning Meditation

Meditation is a great way to start your morning. You can use this time to set your intentions, cleanse your body and mind, and boost vitality. Make it a key part of your wake-up routine, and you'll reap the benefits throughout your day.

Do this: On waking.

You'll need: Nothing but yourself and your bed, and five minutes!

What to do:

1. On waking, give yourself a few minutes to acclimatize to the day. Then take a deep breath in and as you exhale, gently stretch out your arms and legs into a starfish position.

2. Feel the pull of your muscles along each limb and the way your chest expands and opens up.

3. Relax in this position and close your eyes.

4. Continue to breathe deeply.

5. Visualize a silver star situated in the centre of your chest. When you inhale, you draw the light from the star

into your heart. As you exhale, the light travels out to the rest of your body.

6. Focus on the words 'in' and 'out'. 'In' represents the vibrant energy of the star filling your heart, 'out' represents the same energy extending outwards to cleanse your body.

7. Take your time and elongate each breath.

8. Make the word 'in' stretch out in your mind.

9. Make the word 'out' stretch out as you exhale.

10. Don't worry if your head starts to fill with thoughts about the day ahead, acknowledge them and bring your attention back to the star in your chest and your breathing.

Visualize the silver star at any point during your day when you feel you need a boost. The simple act of bringing this to mind, will re-enforce those feelings of rejuvenation.

Meditation Energy Quick Fix

For a quick energy fix, try this mini meditation, which will leave you feeling uplifted and in a positive frame of mind.

Do this: Anytime you need a quick pick-me-up.

You'll need: Five minutes when you can switch off.

What to do:

1. Focus solely on the rhythm of your breathing, so close your eyes and feel the rise and fall of your chest.

2. Slow each breath down and notice how this makes you feel relaxed. Notice too how each breath infuses you with power and energy.

3. Count the breaths as you take them in a 'one...two' rhythm.

4. Leave a bigger gap between the 'one' and the 'two' and notice how your body responds.

5. Don't engage with any thoughts. Let them float through your mind, then bring your attention back to your breathing. When you're ready, open your eyes, and stretch your body out. Roll your shoulders back and lengthen your spine.

THERE IS NO NEED TO RUSH, I FIND THE JOY IN SIMPLY BEING

Wind Down Evening Meditation

The power of meditation is most obvious when it's used to calm the mind. Practiced daily before bed, it will help you release any stress from your body and mind and find the stillness within for a restorative sleep.

Do this: Before bedtime to encourage a good night's sleep, or at the end of a stressful day, when you need a moment of calm.

You'll need: A piece of moonstone, and somewhere comfortable to sit.

What to do:

1. Sit quietly and hold the moonstone in your hands. Let it nestle in your palms and feel the cool, calm energy of the stone against your skin.

2. Close your eyes and imagine that you're floating on a lake beneath the moonlight. The deep blue water is warm and inviting, and you enjoy the sensation of it against your skin.

3. The moon casts its gentle light upon your body, and you feel this healing energy soothing you from head to toe.

4. Hold this image in your mind and relax.

5. For every breath in, focus on the word 'Peace'. Feel it permeate your being.

6. For every breath out, focus on the word 'Release' and let go of any tension that you've been holding on to.

7. Say the words softly in your mind over and over as you inhale and exhale – 'Peace' and 'Release'.

8. If any thoughts sneak into your mind, simply bring your focus back to the lake and the moonlight and concentrate on the breathing words 'Peace' and 'Release'.

9. Continue with this for as long as you need to feel totally relaxed.

10. To finish, place the moonstone beneath your pillow so that its gentle nurturing energy can replenish you as your sleep.

What is mindfulness?

Mindfulness is a practice which helps you retrain your focus on the present moment. By becoming aware of your thoughts, feelings and other sensations, you are able to live in the moment, to connect with the world at a deeper level, and release stress. Research shows that it's a key component to happiness, and has an uplifting effect on the mood, which in turn helps to create more positive energy.

Mindful Energy

Sometimes we need to step outside of ourselves to really appreciate our beauty and strength. This mindful exercise will switch up your perspective by allowing you to become an observer. It clears the mind and allows energy to flow freely.

Do this: Any time of day when you need to recharge.

You'll need: A chair, yourself, and 5 – 10 minutes.

What to do:

1. Sit in the chair in a comfortable position.

2. Slow your breathing down and focus on the rise and fall of your chest.

3. Become aware of your surroundings, and take note of the space, of where you are and other objects around you.

4. Close your eyes and imagine you're outside of your body, looking at yourself.

5. Notice all the wonderful things that make you, you.

6. Feel yourself floating in the space and enjoy the sensation of lightness.

7. Now bring yourself back to your body, sit within your skin and feel its shape around you.

8. Notice how all of your organs work together to imbue you with energy. Notice how your body protects you.

9. Notice too, how every breath fills you with power.

10. Say 'I am strong and empowered.'

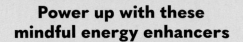

Power up with these mindful energy enhancers

* **Practice mindful eating**
Whenever you eat something, pay attention to each mouthful. Notice how the food feels in your mouth. Think about the texture and the taste. Count each chew slowly, then as you swallow notice how you feel. Focus on the nourishment that your body is receiving.

* **Engage your ears**
Stop and listen. Identify three different sounds. Notice how each one makes you feel in the moment. This exercise brings you into the present moment, helping to ground you.

* **Follow the path of your breath**
Take a moment to follow the path of your breath. Track the journey it takes as you inhale through your nose, and how the air is absorbed by your body.

* Light a candle

Light a candle and spend five minutes focusing
on the flame. Watch it twist and flicker, and let
any thoughts and observations come and go,
as you continue to gaze into the light.

* Focus on an uplifting image

Find a picture, view, or object that you like
looking at. Take a couple of minutes out of
your schedule to appreciate the image.
Relax, and soften your stare. Enjoy the
feelings that arise.

* Stop, breathe, feel

Imagine time is standing still for a minute.
There is no need to act, to move, to do
anything. Ask yourself, 'what do I feel?' Let
any emotions come to the surface and
acknowledge them.

DAILY ENERGY CLOCK

7

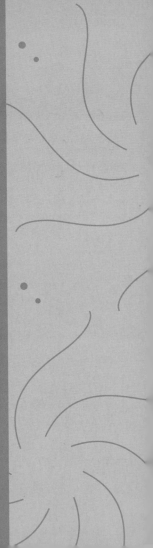

Daily energy helpers

Around the clock vitality is possible, with a few tips and tricks that you can introduce into your daily routine. If you get into the habit of regularly checking in with yourself throughout the day, you'll know when you need a boost or to take some time out.

This daily energy plan is a good starting point and will help you feel empowered and strong. You can adapt any of the suggestions to suit your needs, and even create your own plan using this as a basis, and some of the other techniques in this book.

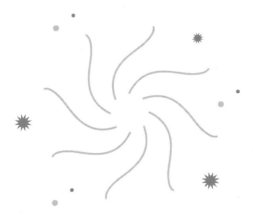

Greet the Day

You might think it doesn't matter what you do first thing, from rolling out of bed, to sleep walking through your usual routine, but this is the time to set a positive empowering tone for the day ahead.

How you greet the day is a game changer. It gives you a solid foundation so that you feel strong and ready to deal with anything that comes your way. A morning meditation, which sets your intention and implants positive suggestions within your subconscious will put a spring in your step and a smile on your face.

Do this: On waking.

You'll need: To set your alarm a couple of minutes earlier than usual so that you can fit this in.

What to do:

1. Sit on the edge of your bed and place your feet firmly on the floor.

2. Roll each foot from the heel to the toe, pushing your sole into the floor so that you can feel your connection with the earth.

3. Close your eyes and picture a blank vista in front of you. The fields roll out in every direction and the sun is peeping over the horizon. The soft morning light kisses your skin and warms you from the inside out.

4. Take a deep breath in and embrace the emptiness. The landscape is a canvas, and you can paint whatever picture you'd like upon it.

5. Think about what you'd like to achieve today and how you'd like to feel.

6. Say 'Today I am powerful. I shine my light and create greatness!'

Mid-morning Pick-me-up

Water is invigorating and has the power to refresh body, mind and spirit. The temperature of the water helps too. Cold water gets the heart pumping, which in turn improves circulation and boosts energy flow.

A quick burst of icy cold water is enough to clear the mind and provide an instant pick-me-up. Couple this with some deep breathing, and you'll feel energized and ready to take on the rest of the day.

Do this: During your morning break.

You'll need: Access to a cold tap.

What to do:

1. Start by running lukewarm water and placing both wrists under the flow. This will probably feel quite comfortable, as you become acclimatized to the temperature.

2. After a few seconds turn off the warm water, pop the plug in the sink and turn on the cold tap.

3. Continue to hold your wrists under the flow and breathe deeply.

4. Imagine drawing that refreshing energy up through each arm and into your chest.

5. Hold your wrists under the tap for at least 30 seconds, then when you're ready, turn the tap off and let both hands rest in the water. Feel the coolness envelope your fingers.

6. To finish, splash a few drops on your face.

THE TIME

IS RIGHT;

THE TIME

IS NOW

Let Go of Lethargy Lunch

The middle of the day is the perfect time to shake things up and go for a short walk. The break in routine, and the different environment will give your brain something new to focus on, particularly if you practice some mindful techniques as you stroll. The gentle exercise gets your heart pumping, and if coupled with some deep breathing, you'll experience an instant energy boost.

Do this: At lunch time.

You'll need: Around 30 minutes to feel the benefits, and somewhere to walk, whether that's your local park, garden or just a quick meander through the nearby streets.

What to do:

1. Start by making sure your posture is correct as you walk. Balance the weight equally between both feet, roll your shoulders back and lengthen your spine so that your chest is open and relaxed.

2. Take deep breaths as you walk, drawing the breath in through you nose, and out through your mouth.

3. Engage all of your senses, so think about what you can see, smell, hear, taste, and feel.

4. Imagine you're a visitor to this planet for the first time and take in every little piece of sensory information.

5. If something grabs your attention, let it. Allow yourself to connect and explore your surroundings.

6. Notice the little things, the sound of leaves rustling in the trees, the feel of the ground beneath your feet.

7. At the end of your walk, take note of how you feel.

Afternoon Lift

The solar plexus is an energy centre, also known as a chakra, situated four finger widths above your belly button. It resembles a whirling ball of light and is associated with the colour yellow. The solar plexus is the seat of self-esteem, and generates personal power, confidence and energy, so it's the perfect chakra to help you power through the afternoon in style.

Do this: Mid-afternoon, or when you take a break.

You'll need: A couple of minutes to yourself to do a quick visualization.

What to do:

1. Rest both hands, one on top of the other, over the solar plexus.

2. Close your eyes and feel the warmth from your palms permeate your belly.

3. Picture a glowing ball of fire, like a tiny sun beneath your hands. Imagine it hovering there, radiating light and warmth.

4. As you inhale, you take in more of the sun's vitality, as you exhale, you draw this light up and into your chest.

5. Continue to breathe and imagine absorbing the fiery ball into your solar plexus.

6. Feel the warmth expand and flood your entire body.

7. Picture yourself as a beacon of light, glowing from head to toe with power.

Tea-time Tincture

Lemon is fresh, zingy, and cleansing and it's the perfect tea-time restorative, after a busy day. If you're not a fan of the fruit, then invest in some lemon essential oil, and sniff the scent for an immediate boost, but if you want to really put the zing back in your swing, then have a go at making this lemony concoction.

Do this: When you finish work.

You'll need: A lemon, some fresh mint, hot water.

What to do:

1. Boil some water in the kettle and place a handful of fresh mint in a teapot, be sure to put one sprig aside for later.

2. Cover the mint with water and let it steep for at least ten minutes. Strain into a jug and pop it in the fridge to cool.

3. Retrieve the minty tea from the fridge and pour into a long glass, add some freshly squeezed lemon juice, then pop the sprig of mint on top.

4. To chill even more, add a couple of ice cubes and sip slowly.

Bedtime Bounty

Before bed is the ideal time to count your blessings. It helps to alleviate anxiety and puts you in the right frame of mind to drift off to sleep. Focusing on something positive before bedtime, is good for the subconscious too.

When your mind is full of happy thoughts, this eventually filters through to your sleeping mind, making you more likely to have lovely dreams and a refreshing sleep.

Do this: Half an hour before bed.

You'll need: A journal and pen, and some lavender essential oil to help you relax.

What to do:

1. Start by massaging a couple of drops of lavender essential oil into your temples. This lovely, scented oil is known for its soothing properties and can be applied directly onto the skin.

2. Gently massage the oil into your temples and forehead until your feel relaxed.

3. Next, take a few minutes to reflect upon your day and

COUNT YOUR BLESSINGS AS YOU COUNT SHEEP

think about the things that you are grateful for. Consider all of the things that have happened and let your thoughts flow.

4. Write down at least three things that you are thankful for. Remember you can choose anything from your morning cuppa to the kind words of a work colleague.

5. Write down as many things as you can. You will probably find that once you start thinking in this way, you'll notice more and more things to be grateful for.

6. When you've finished take a moment to quietly read through everything, before going to bed.